Six Simple Steps

Imagination to Paper

Build

A

World

CANDACE J. THOMAS

SHADESILK
PRESS

S3 Formula™ Books

Write Fight Scenes: The Ultimate Guide That Will Wow Your Readers

Create A Villain: The Essential Role of a Fully Conceived Antagonist

Build A World: Imagination To Paper

The S3 Formula: Publishes A Book in Six Simple Steps

Write A Book: Fit More Words Into Busy Lives

Books by Candace J. Thomas

YOUNG ADULT FANTASY

Vivatera

Conjectrix

Everstar

PARANORMAL SATIRE/COMEDY

Vampire-ish: A Hypochondriac's Tale

NOVELLAS, ANTHOLOGIES, POETRY

The Hawkweed

Moments in Millennia

Wandering Beautiful

Of Snow and Moonlight

WORLD BUILDING

YOU ARE THE OMNIPOTENT CREATOR OF YOUR UNIVERSE

INTRODUCTION:

It's a beautiful world. Lush, green grass sprawls out along the cascading hilltop. The high mountain peaks tower over the little village of small significance. Until the day a stranger arrives and changes the fate of the entire world and sending our protagonist into a daring, perilous adventure.

Are you ready to take the responsibility of creating this world? It's not as simple as drawing a makeshift map in your spiral notebook. Our poor protagonist will find dangers unimagined, travel to different lands, and discover more about himself or herself than they ever expected.

World Building is the corner stone to any speculative fiction novel. Whether it be fantasy, sci-fi, steampunk, ANYTHING—your world building is critical to the success of your novel. It builds depth and believability, not only for the reader, but also for you as the writer, to help you understand the world as your characters would and how to write it. World building is a beautiful experience for any writer.

You've always wanted to play God. Now you get your chance.

BEFORE YOU BUILD

The evolution of a story takes on many phases.

First, you have your idea, usually involving a character or situation, a heroic act, a problem that needs to be solved. This is not always the case, but it was for me. Characters are the key component to your story, and their reaction to the world keeps the story moving.

When placing your characters into the world, you get more of a feel of how they live and breathe in their surroundings. So, sometimes you start to experiment with chapters and situations before your world is really discovered. Don't worry! This is normal. Close to the beginning you will need to stop and create a sustainable, functioning world for your characters to play in. And yes, sometimes this part can drive you crazy, but it can also be loads of fun.

In these Six Simple Steps to world building, you will understand the core essentials that make your world revolve around the sun (or suns, if it were). These steps will take the overwhelming task of developing a sustainable culture for your characters and help give you structure and organization, along with building your confidence in writing your characters and scenes.

You will start to bring your world in to your story, just as you would a character in your novel. The world needs to exist without you and live within the mind of the reader. That is a mark of a truly magical, wonderful world. It's an art of our craft.

Ready to play God? Let's get building.

STEP 1: MYTHOLOGY

I know, you just want to get to the map. Don't worry, the map is coming. But before we start plotting the structure, let's take a look at the Mythology—the reason why this world is here in the first place.

UNDERSTANDING THE GODS

The Mythology is one of the fun bits that helps you tell a thorough story. It's another story within the story. Mythology is the reason why the world is there, and why the story is needed. Just like the mythology of ancient Greece, myths help explain the world around them. Like much of other world building, the mythology may not even show up in your story, but while exploring it, you might find a place for it after all.

Much of your creative lore will come alongside the other steps I'll explain, and that's how it should be. You need a starting point for your creativity and other things will come to you as you create. So, where should you start?

DEITY is a great place to start. A simple decision on your part about the gods of your world can decide the fate of your character. Tell us how it all happened. Think about what the roles were and the story that surrounded the idea to have a world like yours.

WHAT kind of beings are they?
WHAT kind of decisions did they need to make, in order to have a world like this?

Deity can play a part in your world if you let them. In basic role-playing games, a deity or god becomes a part of a cleric or mage and the power they worship or practice. There can also be a religious aspect to the gods you create.

HOW can the deities help this world?

The celestial story is one of very little importance in most works of fiction, so don't focus on it too much, unless you want to incorporate it later into your world.

> *AUTHOR TIP: In my fantasy series, I brought out the mythology to unify what was happening in the final journey of my heroine. It elevated the storytelling and tied it into the beginning, which a good series should do. It helps create author credibility and helps satisfy the readers who were with you in the journey.*

UNDERSTANDING THE PLANET

I'm not asking for you to create an entire planet. We don't need to get into the core, magma, mantle, and crust about it. But what I want you to think about are basic celestial decisions.

The heavens can play a critical role or basically be the stars above. Having two suns on your planet is an identifiable feature, and one that people will remember. In your mythology, you can create a reason why. No one would need to know but you, but your consistency of this feature will be evident in your writing. Just like tracing the stars for navigation, your characters may need to know how to diagram their own chart. Small, insignificant details to the reader can be markers for the writer. The more you understand your heavens, the smoother your writing becomes.

BASIC MECHANICS

Characters don't need to understand how their world works. For them it should feel like magic. But we need some science in with our mythology.

- IF you write about a sea voyage, there needs to be tides.
- IF you write about traveling at night, there needs to be waxing and waning of the moon.

These little mechanics we know in science could be told through mythology of the world. Each of these could have a story behind it.

Imagine if you are telling a story about a traveler at night. Does he picture the moon as a bright bit of rock reflecting the sun or will he know it as a night guardian, protector of travelers, or even a ball of green cheese. If there are stories you create behind these details, your world becomes more real and your writing of your world deepens.

BRINGING IN MAGIC

If you are writing a fantasy world, you may need to incorporate your magic into the mythology. You probably already have. A lot of fantasy stories start with the magic first and then the world. As much as I wish we could all have magic at our fingertips and all you needed to do was snap, that's not the best approach to a magic origin.

MAGIC needs a story as well. Just like a character, magic should have its own story. Understanding its myth is a mark of great storytelling.

MAGIC SYSTEMS do not need to be complicated, but they do need to be figured out. Some authors go to extraneous lengths in their magic systems, diagramming them out, understanding how each component will react with the other. That can be great fun if you enjoy it, but it's not for everyone. But you do need to understand what it can and cannot do.

Here are things to consider:

- Where did it come from?
- Who can wield it?
- How powerful should it be?
- What are the limits?
- What is its purpose in the world?

BE CONSISTENT in your story of magic. Readers are sharp and they will remember. It's best to tackle problems with magic at the very beginning of your world building, especially if you are writing something epic. If you don't understand its role, make the magic forgiving, something moldable or pliable for your story, so the reader isn't suddenly surprised by what just happened, but believe it organically instead. If your magic is rigid, you need to be rigid as well, and your characters will adapt to it. Think about what your characters can do within their magical limitations. Use your own logic and solve the problem.

STEP 2: CARTOGRAPHY—

THE LARGE SCOPE

Now, let's get to the real fun. Are you ready to make a map?

This part has probably been floating in your brain for a while. I bet you've even taken out a spiral notebook and sketched something out, just for your ideas to focus on. I know, I've done it.

ELEMENTARY CONSTRUCTION

With modern technology, you can view any place in the world. You can view the snow-top peaks of the Himalayas or the sands of the Sahara. We are so fortunate, we can escape anywhere if we wish. When creating a world from scratch, consider how the world was formed.

GEOGRAPHY AND GEOLOGY

Many maps have mountains, and why not? Mountains are cool! Mountains can bring perilous journey or escape. Mountains can hide trolls and treasure, orc, elves, goblins, even caves. But there are certain functions of mountains and mountain ranges that you should consider:

- How were they formed?
- Will they be a hindrance to your story?
- What role will the mountains play?

If you place mountains on your map, they become a pivotal role in your story. This gives the readers something to look forward to. Mountains are instantly recognized by a reader looking at a map.

QUICK GEOLOGY LECTURE

Mountains are formed when tectonic plates collide. How the plates collide will determine how they form. The Andes are steep, thrusting one plate under the other. The Himalayas are tall because the plates are crashing into each other, both going up. When forming your mountains, just consider the impact it has made to the environment around it.

Mountains can also be formed from volcanic activity, such as Mount Vesuvius or Krakatoa. Both of these mountains have devastated the environment surrounding them. The way the people live around them has altered their lifestyle and vitality. Volcanos are lonely mountains, angry in their origin. Think back on the mythology and the story it could tell.

Even a little research into some of these or other mountain ranges could be beneficial to your writing. Just an afternoon on usgs.gov or even a Wiki site would do it.

EBBS AND TIDES
And now that you've plopped down your mountains on your map, time to consider water.

Here on Earth, the planet is mostly ocean. Land is immediately what you want to draw on your map, but what is surrounding your piece of land matters, too. Of course, seas and oceans are not as exciting to see as mountains on a map, but they can also hold a lot of adventure.

Sea travel has been a staple in fantasy for hundreds of years. Even Shakespeare used it. Sea travel gives a different perspective to your readers, breaks up the mundane foot voyage, and plays with different directions. Here is where you can use your navigational skills while building your stars. There is also an explorer feel to it, like sailing to a new, undiscovered country.

WATER WAYS
It sounds so easy to just draw a few squiggly lines on a map and title it RIVER, but really think about how and why it is there.

- How can my characters benefit from the river?
- Can you use it for travel?
- Where is the population?

Water is the giver of life. Remember that. Rivers are essential to your world, just as the Nile is to Egypt. Even on a desert planet, water is critical to every civilization. Things grow around water, and that means people live around rivers and lakes. Rivers are a great use for transport—not only for your characters to travel down, but also for trade. In worlds of simple civilization, such as basic fantasy, trade becomes very important.

Think about the direction your river is flowing and be consistent. Most people think downwards when it comes to water, such as ice caps melting and water running down. It's the same on a map. People may automatically make an assumption that the water on your map flows down, from the top of the page to the bottom. If you construct it differently it needs to be explained in your story or otherwise that is the general conclusion.

However you construct it, please think about how to use water in your world.

DESIGNING YOUR PERFECT WORLD

Design can be tricky. Sometimes it takes the skilled hand of a map maker to get everything right.

> *AUTHOR TIP: You can find artists that commission maps on websites like fivrr.com or etsy.com—contact me for a personal recommendation.*

Researching the real world can be fun, if you have time. Learn to evaluate the world around you differently.

HOW DO YOU MEAN?

I recently made muffins. The splatter of the batter as I scoped a spoonful into another cup left an interesting glop. When I baked it, it took the form of a volcano. That was a fun image, something very ordinary that amused me and gave me inspiration. Things like that can help you identify the world you want the story to be in.

Here are some other ideas:

- Spaghetti sauce splatter
- Drying mud puddles
- Anything that leaves an interesting image

Some ideas for storytelling come from looking at your own world differently. Try it and see if it works for you.

STEP 3: BEAUTIFICATION—

THE SMALL SCOPE

Okay, you've got your gods looking down on your world. You've got your world ready to explore. Now, let's make it pretty. Little details can make your world wondrous. For me, it's ALL about the little details and secrets you can add to your world and your story.

PAINT YOUR LANDSCAPE

Our world has such fun and diverse landscapes. You should add all sorts to your world.

- Deserts
- Grassy Fields
- Swamps and Marshes
- Tropics
- Snow Caps

The world is covered with these different landscapes. The small scope is really what the reader will be paying attention to, what they will be identifying with. If you talk about the tropical heat and cascading palms of the trees, most readers can identify the sight and feeling you are evoking through your words. Your job as the writer is to recreate an image that will withstand the entire novel or series. By painting your landscape, you can entice the reader into visualizing your world.

> *AUTHOR TIP: One trick I have learned over the years is to incorporate the five senses into your scenery. By using touch, taste, smell, sight, and sound, you are engaging the reader with things that are familiar. It is not necessary to bring in all five on one page, but don't forget about them. Touching on the senses evoke memory in the reader.*

> *EXAMPLE: The sharp scent of pink peppermints stung a memory of my grandfather smacking the sweet sugar from his lips as he brushed the light candy dust from his fingers.*

SETTING THE STAGE

Really think about the colors and textures of your world. A reader already has a great grasp of what they see and feel every day, so it's time to tap into their sensory memory.

If you plan on changing the look and feel of things in your world, it needs to be very prominently stated near the beginning, or the reader will fill in the gaps with things they already identify with. If in your world the sky is red, you need to state that as a defining feature to the landscape you are introducing to them. Not necessarily the very first line, but in the beginning while you are setting up the character and scene. A detail like this can be a bombshell later and may take the reader out of the story, which you never want to do. When the reader no longer believes, they will lay down the book.

DON'T LET THEM LAY DOWN THE BOOK!

Keep the setting as real as possible, even when you are changing things around. If you give the reader black apples, how will the flavor change from what they are used to? These little details are important. Connect them to what you are trying to achieve.

FINDING THE SECRETS

This is my favorite thing to do. Think about the special places you like in your real life and try to incorporate some of those them. If you like hiking, what makes the hike special? Where would you go if you need to think or dream? These little secrets are what pepper your world.

Secrets also should be incorporated into your story, be part of the adventure. If a magic key is hidden in a cave alongside an ancient mountain, you as the author should know where it

is. Explore your world and figure out certain special places
that you want to show your readers.

Places could include:

- Secret caves
- Hidden places behind waterfalls
- Underground tunnels
- Hilltop stone tables

Let your imagination take over. Let it rove through your map
and explore things that you didn't think of on the Large
Scale. Find the little details and tell their story.

Sometimes secrets come out in the storytelling, things you
never expect that happen out of pure inspiration. When
those do happen, treasure them, and write them down so
you can keep track.

STEP 4: RACE OF LIFE

Your world has air, gods, water, land, and secrets. All it needs now is some life to surround it with wonder. Race here is in reference of different types of people, creatures, or fantasy beings. Your world is big and it needs to be populated with all sorts of life.

HUMANKIND

Many writers stick with what they know—HUMANS. There is nothing wrong with humans. I'm partial to using humans in my novels. Placing people and society around your world is perfectly fine. I mean, look around you and see all the different types of people and personalities that you encounter. The more diversified you make your people, the more fun it becomes for the reader.

If you are stuck I have an activity for you—people-watch. I love people-watching. It's fascinating. Take a notebook and go to the mall. I want you to not only watch the people interacting, but speculate about what brought them here in the first place. I also do this in the airport, where you can find a complete mixed bag of people, each with their own story to tell.

If you are writing fantasy or sci-fi, have fun with your human characters. Using humans makes the writing easier, since you know humans, you ARE one. Adding magic, disabilities, and superpowers in your writing is fun. You can create what you wish you could in real life. This is a great time to think about those other abilities. Don't make it too complicated, but just have fun.

> *AUTHOR TIP: Don't name people in your novel unless you plan on them having a part in your story. If you name them, your reader is making a memory of the person. They will want to know where this person will be in the novel, what part are they going to play. If you refer to them as 'man,' 'mother,' 'boy,' 'teacher,' 'unicorn,' whatever, this doesn't make the same connection and you can move on without losing the reader. They won't care. Too many characters is hard for the reader to follow, so be careful.*

DIVERSITY

I'm excited to see who lives on your world, how the population grows and diversifies, how the animals and people coexist. In most sci-fi and fantasy, not all life is created the same. There is a plethora (that's right, I said plethora) of differing specimens that breathe air and eat food, and they should be different. This is when you get your notebook out and start drawing (if even stick figures) all those creatures or species you'd like to have in your world.

EVOLUTION

Species adapt to the environment they live in. This is true for every environment in our own world; it should be true for any world you create. Whether it be fantasy, sci-fi, or wherever, life will need to find a way to live within its surroundings. For example, if your race of creatures need to swim to catch fish, then give them gills and webbed feet. If you've created mole men who live in caves, then they won't do very well in the sun. Little evolutionary details will be reflected in your writing if you are considerate to your characters' lifestyles.

HOW IT WORKS
Evolution is something that is proven, even though controversial when talking with your Great Aunt Myrtle. Evolution is what has created all the wonderful varieties of life. As a writer, embrace the possibilities that it offers.

Evolution, in simple terms, is the dying out of what doesn't work and reproducing what does. Zebras have stripes because they blur together when they run from predators. This began when a few zebras developed stripes and they survived by tricking their predators. The ones without stripes would get caught and eaten. So, the stronger striped zebras bred together, and eventually the offspring inherited bolder, deeper stripes. Very basic, easy terms.

In your world, the same type of things can happen, without writing years and years of history. Just use your logic.

DETAILS OF A SPECIES

In previously written stories with mythical creatures, we can analyze some of the evolutionary advances. In early fantasy, Elves were given pointy ears, so that they could hear things from many miles away. Dwarves were good at mining because of their incredible night vision. You can bring little details to your own species and evolution in your world. Again, just, be consistent with what you do.

Look at your world and decide what evolution has happened to those people over thousands of years. What would happen to people if they lived in swampy marshlands and never left? How do you think their skin would look?

CREATIVITY

I can't stress this enough. When creating your own species, please be creative. We are so used to the fantasy species tropes that elves should be tall and beautiful, but I also remember elves being something you see on the side of a box of crackers.

> *AUTHOR TIP: One of the worst things that I ever read about my own writing was that it was derivative (meaning unoriginal, or copied from other works). I hated that statement because I tried so hard to do something different. I know the difficulties of being original, but pushing creativity is worth to make it stand out. Seek*

opportunities to make your work be the one that people envy and wish they had thought of.

POPULATING THE GLOBE

Now, I want you to pull out your map and study it. Where are you going to place all these different types of people, animals, or whatever you want to create?

- What kind of people are going to live in your desert?
- Who are going to live near your oceans?
- Who would ever live in the snowcapped mountains?

Think about the people, name them, and think about their culture and society. If I were you (which I have been), I would even go as far as drawing a bit, searching Wiki sites, artist sites, even Pinterest.com. There is so much creativity out there and you have the internet to help.

FANTASY BEINGS

You can research any of these creatures on a Wiki site or elsewhere on the internet or in a book. Here is a rough guide for you to jumpstart your writing.

ELVES	DWARVES	GOBLINS
ORCS	VAMPIRES	HARPIES
SIRENS	TROLLS	DRAGONS
FAIRIES	NYMPHS	SPRITES
PIXIES	WEREWOLVES	GIANTS

STEP 5: CIVILIZATION AND GOVERNMENT

With people populations, there needs to be some sort of authority in society. Whether it be Monarchy rule or Tribal Council, people need to be governed, and this gives you a great opportunity to explore more about the people you just set loose in your world.

GOVERNMENT

All around the globe there are different types of government. Who do you want ruling your world? Many plots incorporate monarchy or government, the prince or castle or guards in some way. Who governs could be a big deal to readers. If you are not writing about such things, still think about who's in charge of this place. It may matter at some point in your novel.

DIFFERENT EXAMPLES OF GOVERNMENT

Here is a list of popular governing systems I've researched. Any can be researched and used in your story in some way or another.

- MONARCHY—Governed by a King or Queen, sometimes called Emperor.
- PRINCIPALITY—Governed by a Prince or Princess.
- REPUBLIC or DEMOCRACY—This is where the people govern, usually with an elected leader.
- ARISTOCRACY—Ruled by the wealthy, the nobility, or the educated.
- DICTATORSHIP—Ruled by one leader who makes absolute decisions on how to rule over the people.

This is just some suggestions on what you might want to do in your world. This doesn't discuss anything tribal or third world cultures, but those are usually kept within their own communities and are not broadly controlled like with the above-listed systems.

ARMIES

Whichever governing body you decide to go with, you will need an army. To be honest, I am not familiar with rank, and when I first started writing fantasy, my novice showed. Here is a quick guide to rank within the US Army (Military.com), so you understand more about where to place your officers.

OFFICERS

2nd Lieutenant> 1st Lieutenant> Captain> Major> Lieutenant Colonel> Colonel

GENERALS

Brigadier General> Major General> Lieutenant General> General

Not that you need these, but it is a good idea to know that rank is important when creating your military. However you want to put your ranking together is really your business, but you need to keep it consistent.

AUTHOR TIP: In my fantasy series, I organized the King's army like this: Guard> Soldier> Major> Captain> Commander. In my Dystopia, I researched the Russian army ranks and placed my protag in the lowest junior class.

COEXISTING

You can look at the rather civilized Europeans traveling to the Northern Americas and finding tribal customs. These were two groups of people existing at the same time, with very different views of their world. This can be the same in world building. Some societies should be more advanced than others. Not everyone should be on the same level of technology. Give your different races their own customs and traditions, their own evolution.

UTOPIAN VS. DYSTOPIAN VS. POST-APOCALYPTIC

Several novels in the twentieth century introduced us to a perfect society, where everyone thinks and acts and believes the same. This is called a UTOPIAN Society—a perfect, harmonious existence, possibly where everyone wears the same clothes and eats the same food. . . . In other words, completely boring. A perfect Utopia is very uninteresting, but depending on what your story needs, could be a great setting for something interesting to perpetuate.

DYSTOPIAN is in the best terms—Anti-Utopia. In this kind of society, things are frightening, usually government controlled and repressive. Dystopian fiction has seen a lot of attention as the Future Us, living under new control. A good story here would be a hero story of rising above the repression for freedom.

When society and government eventually fails, or the world is in a post-war collapse, this is where POST-APOCOLYPTIC is seen. This is returning your world back to its bare state, but still with some modern technologies. It's a grungy, dirty world of survival. Many stories here are of searching for basic needs—clean water, toilet paper, whatever you can think of. It's a beat-up world and frightening as hell.

THE CLASS SYSTEM

Not all people live equally, especially in fiction. Class is a prevalent theme in many of our favorite classic novels. As much as we would like to live equally in real life, there still should be a variety of people and wealth. Farmers would not be treated the same as rich landowners. Just remember your story and who it involves. Understanding the community in which they were raised is critical to good storytelling. Even if only a few lines get into the finished work, the preparation helps smooth out the writing in general.

CURRENCY

In every governing body, there is some sort of money system, or a way to trade services for goods. Don't forget the monies. Come up with your own system, and be consistent. Look at your world and see what fits.

In fantasy novels, we see the bartering goods for money or services, people exchanging their crafts for something. There is always a need for supplies on an epic journey. This can be a great place to develop characters and relationships.

If it's selling junk scraps for a portion of food, that makes it more of a plot item. It would be a focus specifically for the characters. It doesn't need to be the main focus, but an important plot point. Look at what your world needs and what its people need to survive.

Looking at our modern currency, everything is going digital. For you sci-fi writers, try and expand your thoughts about how money is spent, used, transferred, all of it. Paper and coin money is disappearing, so think creatively about the money situation.

Don't forget to have fun with it. Gold is so boring. Naming money is as fun as anything else in your world. Look at other currency around our world, how it's shapes, different names, for reference. The value is only what you make it.

BUILDING YOUR CULTURE

Culture is an excellent opportunity for you to add a unique history to people. In every civilization, people have customs, traditions, and holidays where they celebrate who they are and where they come from.

Look at your own nationality and history. There is a fun, complex story there, wherever you are from. My heritage points me back to Norway, Denmark, and England. Their dress and celebrations were something that has always fascinated me. The dialect, the language, the rich colors of their flag—these are all something that you can look at and add to your culture. Make your people special.

This is something not many writers think about, focusing on the adventure and their character, because not much culture might show up in your story. But I think you would be surprised. If you add culture, there will be pride in your work and I'm sure it will show up. You are creating years of traditions, and the deeper you go, the better your understanding will be of these people you are writing about. It's such a fun way to spend an afternoon.

STEP 6: PLACING YOUR CHARACTER

And now is the exciting part—writing your world. So much preparation has now gone into your world that you can see the mountains and smell the flowers. The people are now living on the land, cultivating the ground, beautifying everything around them. There are castles and cyborgs, water sprites and pixies, dragons, beasts, and ruthless rulers.

It's time for the adventure to start.

READY, SET, GO!

You have just completed a ton of research and work on your new world and I don't want your hard work to go to waste. You know your world better than any reader will, but how do you incorporate the world building without saturating your audience?

Very carefully.

SCENE

I want you to blend your original concept, even the first pages or chapters you've already written, into the rich world you've created.

Blending can be hard if you have already started. I would suggest go over those first pages and add some details in gentle ways. Simple literary tricks and narrative techniques can help paint the world around your characters.

My favorites:

- Alliteration (similar use of letters or sounds in the same sentence)
- Personification (life to the lifeless)
- Imagery (descriptive words)
- Sensory (using the 5 senses)

TECHNIQUE

SETTING DRIVEN VS. CHARACTER DRIVEN
In my own words, I feel there are two ways a person writes:

- **Setting Driven** – allows the setting to direct the characters. Writers like NEIL GAIMAN, JANET LEE CAREY, and SHANNON HALE are Setting Driven writers—Storyteller style
- **Character Driven** – drives the characters into the setting. Authors like MARIA V. SNYDER, SUZANNE COLLINS, and VERONICA ROTH are Character Driven writers—Revealing style

There is nothing wrong with either, just recognize your own writing style and run with it. The difference when reflecting your world building is the way you present the world to the audience. I recognize that I am a **Character Driven** writer. I let the characters' decisions drive the plot along. What they see and how they end up there is where you see a lot of my world building. **Setting Driven** writers start with introducing you to the unique world first before allowing the characters to decide anything.

Evaluate some of your favorite authors and their unique storytelling and look at your own writing. This will help you along your way with what information you need to divulge about your set-up.

FIRST PAGE

You may hear this from other places, not just me—your first page is critical. A lot of the time your first FIRST page will not be your final FIRST page, if that makes sense. It may take a few drafts to understand exactly what you want to tell on your first page.

REMINDERS

Be proud of the world you've created. It looks FANTASTIC. I have some personal advice to give you:

- Your Mythology might be ancient by the time your story starts. Remember how old it is. Like our language has Latin roots, but it's not something we think about every day. Let it play a role, but in its own way.

- Your mountains are millions of years old too. They are witnessed to all the change of landscape, the wars, the celebrations. They are the sentinels of truth to your world. Use the banding of bedrock to tell a little history of the world and how it got to this story.
- Every tree matters. Every bloom exists. Whether it be on page or just in your mind. Your world is so beautiful. Live in it.
- Use your logic to problem-solve your world. It is as difficult to fix as our own. Treat it like the real thing.
- Use sensory perception to let the reader into your word. What they see and feel and smell and hear all matters.
- Plant secrets in your world. Readers love secrets. Especially in epic storytelling.
- Most importantly – Be Consistent. Take notes. Keep notes. Add notes. The better you are with consistency, the more it shows in your writing and in your world. It truly makes a difference.

THE HEART OF AN ARTIST

The simple and beautiful art of building a world is a fantastic achievement. Be very proud of what you just did. It's quite amazing. Don't feel bad if every detail doesn't get page time; it reflects in your writing and quality as a writer.

The act of world building makes your job as the storyteller easier. It gives your characters an engaging world that is theirs to explore. The more time and detail you add in your pre-build, the easier the story will flow. You know more about the world so just let the story tell you where it needs to go.

Writing is the most fulfilling art. An author takes words and paints pictures that no one can see but the reader. Each reader sees a different image, but it is the same words making the magic. Creating beautiful, streaming sentences is truly marvelous. Writing affects people's emotions and stimulates their brains so that they feel the adventure. A simple string of words can tell the most amazing things: words that fill the soul and thrum the heart. It's the most romantic, most terrifying, most amazing art there is.

Be proud to be that artist YOU.

There is nothing better than creating MAG

ABOUT THE AUTHOR

Candace J. Thomas is an award-winning author of fantasy and sci-fi, as well as a freelance editor. She has been a featured instructor at LTUE: Life, The Universe, and Everything Sci-fi and Fantasy Writer's Symposium (ltue.net), League of Utah Writers (luwriters.com), and classrooms around the Wasatch Front. Check out her award-winning fantasy series: The Vivatera Series, and her vampire satire Vampire-ish: A Hypochondriac's Tale.

When she's not being an omnipotent world builder, Candace can be found eating Count Chocula and avoiding laundry.

You can find her books at her website: candacejthomas.com

www.ingramcontent.com/pod-product-compliance
Lightning Source LLC
Chambersburg PA
CBHW051129250726
48655CB00007B/2971